How Do Animals Use Their Five Senses?

Alejandro Algarra / Rocio Bonilla

BARRON'S

"Kate, do you think animals use the five senses just like we do?" asks Jack.

"I was just trying to find out how ducks find food, because I don't think they can smell with their bills!" says Kate.

"What about cats—can they see in the dark?" wonders Jack.

"We should look this up!" suggests Kate.

3

Smell

Sight

Taste

Touch

4

Hearing

The senses in the animal kingdom

Animals use their senses to respond to their surroundings. They use hearing, touch, sight, taste, and smell in many ways. They can see light, color, and motion, and they can hear sounds, tell apart different flavors and smells, and sense cold and heat. Animals can even feel vibrations! When an animal uses its senses, it has all the information it needs to survive. For example, the fox can smell if an enemy is coming, like a bear, and knows that it needs to flee or hide for safety.

Sight: Light and motion

Sight is a very important sense. With their eyes, animals can see both light and motion. Some animals can also see the colors, shapes, and sizes of objects in their surroundings. They also use their eyes to see how their surroundings are changing. They can see movements and changes in color and shape, and even changes in how far away something is (useful when hunting). The animals with the best sense of sight are predators—animals that hunt other animals—like brown bears and cheetahs.

Seeing and not being seen

Many of us share our homes with one of the best night hunters in the entire animal kingdom—the cat! Cats can sense light and motion when it's almost completely dark, so they can hunt at night without being seen. Poor mice! But, our pets aren't the only cats with night vision. Large wild cats like lions and tigers use their incredible sense of sight to hunt at night, too. Other animals, like birds, have amazing eyesight during the day. Falcons can see a mouse move from more than one mile away!

Two eyes, eight eyes, a thousand eyes

Some animals have round pupils, while others have more oval-shaped pupils. Eye color also varies: there are red, blue, yellow, green, and black eyes. There are very simple eyes that only sense changes in light, and very complex eyes, like those of insects. Is it normal to have two eyes? It is for frogs, horses, and snakes, but not for spiders. They can have up to eight eyes. Giant clams can have more than a thousand!

Can you hear me now?

Sounds are sent out by vibrations through the air, water, or ground. Animals use their sense of hearing not only to find food but also to flee from their enemies. Another very important purpose of this sense is to hear the sounds made by other animals. For example, a mother bird can hear her chicks chirping when they're hungry so she knows it's time to feed them. Meerkats use warning cries to alert the group to different types of hunters so they can hide.

Owl's ears

Owls have an excellent sense of hearing. The round, flat shape of their face helps them to better sense the tiniest movements of their prey. In fact, they can hear a small rodent or mouse rustle in the leaves, or even under snow. This is why they are such great hunters in the dark. But, many rodents, like mice, are not totally defenseless. They also have excellent hearing and sometimes manage to escape.

Other ways to hear

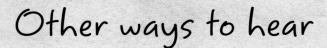

Sound is sent more quickly through water than through air. Whales, such as humpback whales, use songs to communicate. Their songs can travel thousands of miles in the ocean to reach fellow whales! Dolphins also use sound to communicate, but they can even use it to find food. They release cries, which we cannot hear, that bounce off nearby objects to create an echo. They measure the time it takes for the echo to return to them, which tells them where the food is! This process is called echolocation. How amazing!

A scent detector

The sense of smell helps animals find food, find a mate, or detect their enemies. Dogs have an incredible sense of smell—it is a thousand times better than ours! Smells travel through the air and are picked up by the nostrils, which are protected inside the nose in some animals. Others, however, have no nose at all. Have you ever seen a jellyfish with a nose?

Superhero sense of smell

Large hunters, like wolves, have an outstanding sense of smell. Wolves can sense smells up to one mile away! They can also smell scents left by other animals many days earlier. Wolves mark their own scent on trees and trails. They do this to communicate with their wolf pack and to mark their territory—the area in which they live—to tell other wolf packs to stay away!

Amazing antennae

Many insects use antennae to smell. Antennae are two feelers located on the head of insects. They come in a variety of shapes and sizes and have tiny, almost invisible hairs that are very sensitive to smells. Ants use antennae to find food, to communicate with fellow ants, to navigate, and to tell the difference between friends and enemies. For ants, antennae are more important than eyes!

What does this taste like?

The sense of taste is used to recognize flavors. There are basic flavors, including sweet, salty, sour, and bitter. Thanks to the sense of taste, animals can tell if their food is nutritious or poisonous. Many animals use their tongues to taste, but not all animals can taste well. Some birds do not have a good sense of taste, and cats cannot taste sweet flavors. No cupcakes for them!

Taste buds aren't just for tongues!

The catfish is a champion taster! Its entire body, including its whiskers, is covered by thousands of taste buds—like the ones we have on our tongues. But, they have twice as many as we do! Flies don't use their entire body to taste—they taste with their feet! They can tell what their food tastes like just by standing on it. Ever wonder why flies always land on your sweet treats? They are able to taste sugar 10 million times better than we can! Butterflies can also taste with their feet. They do this to find nectar to eat and to find the perfect leaf on which to lay their eggs. By standing on a leaf, they can taste it to see if the caterpillars—which will hatch from their eggs—will be able to eat it.

Very touching

The sense of touch allows animals to gather lots of information about the world around them. Not only is it used to tell the shape and size of things, but it also lets animals know whether things are cold or hot or smooth or rough. The sense of touch is located in the skin, but some areas of the body are more sensitive than others. The skin on the lips and hands of primates, like monkeys and humans, is very sensitive. But dogs, cats, and seals use their muzzles and whiskers to feel things.

Touching to eat

Duck bills are incredibly sensitive to touch. Ducks can feel with their bills just like we do with our fingers! When ducks dive under the water, they reach the bottom and bury their bills in the mud. Although they can't see anything, they can feel even the smallest movement with their bills. This is how they catch the small worms that they eat.

There aren't just five senses...

Some animals don't have all of the five senses mentioned, but they make up for it with other senses that we cannot even imagine. Snakes, for example, can't hear. Rattlesnakes cannot even hear the noise they make with their own tails. However, they can sense infrared rays, which means that they can "see" heat. This is how, even at night in the desert, they can tell whether what is in front of them is a cold stone or a poor, frightened mouse.

"Kate, I can taste and smell better than you!" brags Jack.

"Well, I can see and hear better than you can!" replies Kate.

"Well, I smell cupcakes in the kitchen!" says Jack.

"Yummy! Let's go!" shouts Kate.

Parent guide

There are five primary senses in the animal kingdom. However, these senses are not developed equally in all animals. As they adapt to their environment, each species uses the senses that can best help them to survive in nature. For example, animals that hunt to eat have senses that are more highly developed to allow them to find prey quickly. These include cats with their night vision, owls with their outstanding sense of hearing, and sharks with their exceptional sense of smell. To defend themselves, many animals that are the prey of these predators are capable of detecting them thanks to their senses. Many herbivores, like zebras and gazelles, have eyes on the sides of their head to see if an animal is approaching them from the rear. Their sense of smell is also very refined, and their ears, which can move independent of each other, allow them to direct their sense of hearing 360 degrees. In the bug world, the senses play an extremely important role in the search for food and a mate, and in communicating with fellow bugs. Insects' antennae are used as organs to smell, touch, and taste. They are covered with countless microscopic hairs, some of which are sensitive to flavors and scents and others to touch. Ants are champion communicators thanks to the scents they leave for other ants.

It is important to explain to children that animals do not see, hear, smell, taste, and touch the same way we do. Insects see things that human beings cannot perceive. For example, some insects can detect ultraviolet rays or polarized light. Plus, the images that their brains make look more like a mosaic pattern—much different than the way our brains interpret images. The majority of animals do not detect colors, or they only see a few of them. Even more incredible are the senses that human beings cannot even imagine, such as seeing heat, feeling magnetism, or detecting electricity.

THE INCREDIBLE SENSES IN THE ANIMAL WORLD

The largest eye in the animal kingdom is found on the giant squid: each of its two eyes can measure 12 inches (30 cm) in diameter or more. These eyes allow them to see in extremely poor light conditions, because they live in the depths of the oceans, thousands of feet under the surface.

Among mammals, the tarsier monkey holds the record for having the largest eyes compared to its face size. If human beings had eyes that size, they would be as large as grapefruits. The tarsier monkey has outstanding night vision, which allows it to hunt for insects, reptiles, and birds.

The compound eyes of predatory insects like the dragonfly may contain up to 30,000 lenses, each of which is capable of capturing light and comprising a tiny part of the whole image. Plus, because of their shape, the eyes of dragonflies and other insects like flies allow them to see almost 360 degrees. Although the images made by insects' eyes are not as clear as ours, they are much better at detecting even the slightest movements.

The bat's ability to pick up ultrasound is widely known. These animals are constantly issuing cries that the human ear cannot detect. They hear the echo of these cries as they bounce off surrounding objects. This makes them capable of avoiding obstacles at high speeds or hunting tiny moths and mosquitoes. And, they can do all of this in total darkness.

Less well-known are some animals' ability to detect low frequency sounds that are inaudible to us. With the help of receptors located in their feet and trunks, elephants are capable of hearing the vibrations of the ground and knowing whether a storm or earthquake is coming. Plus, other elephants that are located miles away can communicate with them via the ground.

The smelling champions, at least on dry land, are bears. Their large noses have folds inside that are covered with thousands of scent sensors. This allows them to detect their food from several miles away or through a foot of snow (the polar bear), and they can even smell leftover food in water.

Sharks have a sense of smell so powerful that humans cannot even imagine it. They are capable of smelling a single drop of blood up to one mile away.

Among insects, the smelling champion is the male silk moth. With its feather-shaped antennae, it is capable of detecting a single scent particle (called a pheromone), which the females give off when they leave their cocoon, at a distance of 6 miles (9 km) or more.

Snakes lack flavor receptors on their tongues. To detect scent and flavor of their prey, they flick their tongue in and out of their mouths, a gesture that has made them famous. In this way, they bring the scent and flavor particles that adhere to their tongues to their palate. Their palate has a special organ, called the Jacobson organ, that captures all the smell and taste information.

The manatee is one of the mammals with the most highly developed sense of touch. Its entire body is covered with fine hairs that function like a cat's whiskers. The manatee uses the hairs to feel small changes in sea currents and to understand the shape of their environment.

Crocodiles have thousands of touch sensors along their jaws and mouth. These receptors allow them to detect movements in water and to detect the location of vibrations. They can sense the tiny vibration that's emitted when a prey drinks on the banks of a river where the crocodile inhabits.

First edition for the United States and Canada published in 2016 by Barron's Educational Series, Inc.

© Gemser Publications, S.L. 2015
El Castell, 38 08329 Teiá (Barcelona, Spain)
www.mercedesros.com

Text: Alejandro Algarra
Design and layout: Estudi Guasch, S.L.
Illustration: Rocio Bonilla

All inquiries should be addressed to:
Barron's Educational Series, Inc.
250 Wireless Boulevard
Hauppauge, NY 11788
www.barronseduc.com

ISBN: 978-1-4380-0891-2

Library of Congress Control No.: 2016930603

Date of Manufacture: April 2016
Manufactured by: L. Rex Printing Company Limited, Dongguan City, Guangdong, China

Printed in China
9 8 7 6 5 4 3 2 1